NORTH MACEDONIA THROUGH THE AGES

A CONCISE GUIDE

By

Martin Miller-Yianni

The Emblem of North Macedonia

i

COPYRIGHT AND ACKNOWLEDGEMENTS

Publisher: Martin Miller-Yianni, Yambol, Bulgaria

First Printed Edition 2023

ISBN 978-619-7742-25-1 (paperback)

ISBN 978-619-7742-26-8 (ePub)

A CIP catalogue record for this book is available from:

The National Register of Published Books in Bulgaria

bulevard 'Vasil Levski' 88,

1504 Sofia,

Bulgaria

Cover Photograph (Stone Bridge, Skopje)

by Fisnik Murtezi on Unsplash.com

CONTENTS

"North Macedonia Through the Ages: A Concise Guide" is an invaluable resource for students, curious travellers, and anyone eager to delve into the history of North Macedonia. As part of a series of books exploring the histories of various countries, it offers a well-organised structure and clear presentation, facilitating easy navigation through different historical periods and chapters, enabling readers to swiftly locate specific information.

From the ancient civilisations of North Macedonia to contemporary developments, this book comprehensively covers the essential facets of the nation's history. It enables readers to grasp the historical context and cultural heritage of the region. Its concise format makes it an ideal choice for those seeking a quick reference or an introduction to North Macedonia's past.

The book offers a comprehensive overview without compromising on accuracy or depth, presented in a readable and accessible British English style. This makes it an excellent resource for gaining knowledge about North Macedonia's diverse historical foundations.

It's worth noting that some chapters may recap important events. Such recapitulations are inevitable, as era transitions often share events and important figures, reinforcing the interconnectedness of North Macedonia's history. They serve as valuable reminders, aiding in comprehending the broader historical narrative.

Whether you wish to refresh your knowledge of a specific historical era or develop a general understanding of North Macedonia's past, this book delivers reliable information and serves as an invaluable guide. It immerses readers in the triumphs, challenges, and cultural metamorphoses that have contributed to North Macedonia's identity, offering a fascinating journey through time.

"North Macedonia Through the Ages: A Concise Guide" is an engaging and informative book that provides a succinct yet comprehensive look at the nation's history. It is an exceptional resource for anyone eager to explore the fascinating story of this region and gain a deeper appreciation for its rich cultural heritage.

The North Macedonian flag features a striking and distinctive design. It consists of a red field, symbolising the valour and courage of the Macedonian people. In the centre, there is a golden sun with eight broadening rays, which is called the Sun of Vergina. This symbol represents the ancient symbol of the Macedonian royal dynasty of the same name.

The eight rays of the sun are pointed alternately towards the edges of the flag, giving it a balanced and harmonious appearance. The golden colour of the sun stands for the richness of the country's cultural and historical heritage. This powerful symbol has deep historical and cultural significance for the North Macedonian people and represents the continuity of their identity and heritage.

The flag was officially adopted on October 5, 1995, following the country's independence from the former Yugoslavia. Its design reflects the nation's rich history and is a source of pride for the North Macedonian people, serving as a powerful emblem of their unity and identity.

North Macedonia spans approximately 34,000 square kilometres and is primarily located in the northern part of Greece. It is characterised by diverse terrain, featuring sprawling mountains, fertile valleys, and rivers. The Balkan Mountain range, including peaks like Mount Olympus, adds to its picturesque landscape. The Vardar, one of the major rivers, meanders through the region, enhancing its agricultural productivity.

With its varied demographic composition, Macedonia has been home to diverse ethnic groups, contributing to its rich cultural network. The region is bordered by Kosovo and Serbia to the north, Bulgaria to the east, Greece to the south, and Albania to the west. Its strategic location has facilitated historical exchanges and cultural influences with these neighbouring countries, enriching its historical significance and geopolitical importance in the broader European context.

The land now known as North Macedonia boasts a rich and diverse ancient history that predates recorded civilisation, with archaeological evidence suggesting human activity dating back approximately 700,000 years to the Paleolithic era. The Neolithic period, around the same time, saw the emergence of organised society and culture, with the region inhabited by various ancient cultures, including the Thracians, Illyrians, and Dardanians.

During this time, the ancient kingdom of Paeonia arose in the 7th century B.C., renowned for its skilled metalworking and active involvement in regional trade, interacting with civilisations such as the Greeks and Thracians. The Paeonians' cultural exchanges contributed to the flourishing of their society, with their distinctive craftsmanship in metalwork, particularly jewellery and weapons, adding to their renown and economic prosperity.

In the southern parts of the region, the ancient kingdom of Dardania, inhabited by Illyrian tribes, displayed significant military prowess and engaged in conflicts with neighbouring powers, including the Roman Republic. The Dardanian capital at Naissus (modern Niš in Serbia) served as a strategic stronghold for trade routes and economic exchanges.

Adjacent to the Dardanian kingdom, the ancient Macedonians, under the leadership of King Philip II, expanded their influence during the 4th century B.C. Philip II's reign saw the restructuring of the Macedonian army, political reforms, and diplomatic ties with neighbouring Greek city-states, leading to the unification of the Greek city-states under Macedonian hegemony after the Battle of Chaeronea in 338 B.C. This victory solidified Macedon's dominance in the Greek world, setting the stage for his son, Alexander the Great, to create one of the most extensive empires in ancient history.

In the later 6th century B.C., the Achaemenid Persians, led by Darius the Great, extended their dominion over the region, bringing about a period of administrative restructuring and cultural assimilation. Persian influence led to the fortification of trade routes, the development of urban centres, and the construction of grand architectural projects that reflected the empire's opulence.

Despite the Persian hold, the region eventually witnessed a resurgence of local autonomy and diverse geopolitical influences following the withdrawal of Persian forces, a pivotal event that marked a new era in the region's history. These ancient roots of North Macedonia, characterised by diverse cultures and the emergence of powerful kingdoms, shaped the cultural, political, and societal landscape for centuries to come, leaving a lasting imprint on the region's rich and varied heritage.

NOTABLE FIGURES OF ANCIENT MACEDONIA

King Perdiccas I: Considered one of the earliest known rulers of ancient Macedonia, King Perdiccas I is credited with laying the foundations of the Macedonian kingdom. His reign marked a significant shift towards a more centralised political system and the consolidation of various tribal communities under a unified authority.

King Alexander I (Alexander the Great): Known for his diplomatic prowess, King Alexander I played a crucial role in maintaining Macedonia's autonomy while navigating the complex power dynamics between the Greek city-states and the Persian Empire. His involvement in the Persian Wars solidified the kingdom's position in the Hellenic world and set the stage for future expansions.

Queen Eurydice I: Renowned for her political acumen and strategic influence, Queen Eurydice I was instrumental in fostering alliances with neighbouring regions, consolidating the kingdom's power base, and promoting cultural development within the Macedonian court.

SIGNIFICANT PLACES IN ANCIENT MACEDONIA

Aegae (Aigai): The ancient capital of the Macedonian kingdom, Aegae, served as the ceremonial and administrative centre of power for early Macedonian kings. The city was home to the royal palace, where important political and religious ceremonies took place, solidifying the region's cultural and political identity.

Pella: Emerging as the capital under the reign of King Archelaus I, Pella became the vibrant hub of Macedonian political and cultural life. It served as a flourishing centre for art, education, and commerce, showcasing the progressive cultural development and prosperity of ancient Macedonia.

Ancient City of Pella

Vergina (Aigai): The burial site of numerous Macedonian kings, including Philip II, father of Alexander the Great, Vergina holds significant archaeological importance, offering valuable insights into the cultural and funerary practices of ancient Macedonian royalty. Its discoveries have contributed substantially to our understanding of the early Macedonian kingdom and its regal heritage.

Tomb of Philip II in Vergina

The period following the reign of King Philip II marked a significant transformation for the kingdom of Macedon as it transitioned from an independent power to a Roman province. After the assassination of Philip II in 336 B.C., his son Alexander the Great assumed the throne, embarking on a series of military campaigns that reshaped the ancient world.

King Philip II

In 334 B.C., Alexander the Great initiated his conquest of the Persian Empire, culminating in his triumph at the Battle of

Gaugamela in 331 B.C. His campaigns resulted in the rapid expansion of Macedonian influence, creating an extensive empire stretching from Greece to India. During his rule, Alexander laid the groundwork for the dissemination of Hellenistic culture, facilitating the fusion of Greek and local traditions in the conquered regions.

Alexander the Great (Alexander I)

Amidst their valorous pursuits, the Macedonians cultivated rich traditions, from their distinctive rituals that paid homage to the ancient ods of Olympus, to their intricate artistic expressions that adorned the walls of their grand palaces. Their appreciation for the arts mirrored the complexities of their societal fabric, weaving together a narrative that celebrated the beauty of human expression amidst the tumultuous backdrop of historical upheaval.

Twelve Gods of Olympus

Following Alexander's death in 323 B.C., his empire was divided among his generals, leading to the Wars of the Diadochi, a period of political fragmentation. The division resulted in the emergence of several Hellenistic kingdoms, with Macedon playing a significant role in the power struggle among Alexander's former generals.

During the 3rd and 2nd centuries B.C., Macedon faced challenges from neighbouring Hellenistic kingdoms and invasions by Celtic tribes from the north. In 168 B.C., the Roman Republic, led by the consul Lucius Aemilius Paullus, defeated the forces of the last Macedonian king, Perseus, at the Battle of Pydna. This event marked the end of Macedonian independence and the commencement of its integration as a Roman province.

The transition from an independent kingdom to a Roman province represented a crucial moment in the region's history, symbolizing the conclusion of the Macedonian monarchy and the start of a new era under Roman rule. The period witnessed the spread of Hellenistic culture and Roman influence, leaving an enduring imprint on the region's language, architecture, and governance.

In 336 B.C., Philip II of Macedon solidified his control over Upper Macedonia, setting the stage for the achievements of his son, Alexander the Great. Alexander's military campaigns resulted in the incorporation of a significant portion of the remaining territories into his vast empire, reshaping the geopolitical landscape and leaving a lasting legacy.

Subsequently, the Romans extended their influence, incorporating most of the Republic into the province of Macedonia, while the northern sectors, including Dardania, fell within the boundaries of Moesia. During the reign of Diocletian, the Roman territories underwent subdivision, leading to the emergence of Macedonia Salutaris and Moesia Prima as distinct administrative units, solidifying Roman presence in the Balkans.

As the 5th century CE approached, historical records concerning the Slavic presence in the region became scarce, contributing to a relative lack of information regarding their early activities and cultural developments. This historical ambiguity laid the groundwork for a complex interplay of cultural evolution that unfolded in subsequent centuries, leaving a profound mark on the historical narrative of the Balkan Peninsula.

During the Migration Period, the expansive territory delineated by the Jireček Line became a melting pot of diverse ethnic groups and cultural influences. Among the populace were individuals with origins stemming from the realms of Thraco-Roman and Illyro-Roman heritage, alongside the presence of Hellenised denisens aligned with the Byzantine Empire and Byzantine Greeks. The region bore the intricate legacy of ancient Thraco-Illyrian languages that had long faded into obscurity prior to the arrival of the Slavic communities. The cultural impact of these earlier inhabitants was significantly eroded by successive waves of barbaric incursions that plagued the Balkans during the early Middle Ages, perpetuating a cycle of Hellenisation, Romanisation, and eventual Slavic assimilation.

In the 6th century, South Slavic tribes began to establish settlements within the borders of what is now North Macedonia, ushering in a new era in the region's cultural narrative. Byzantine Greek historians referred to these Slavic settlements as "Sclavenes," who were active participants in various assaults against the Byzantine Empire, either autonomously or in conjunction with the Bulgars or Avars.

King Perdiccas I: As already mentioned, he one of the earliest known rulers of ancient Macedonia, King Perdiccas I is credited with laying the foundations of the Macedonian kingdom. His reign marked a significant shift towards a more centralised political system and the consolidation of various tribal communities under a unified authority.

King Alexander I (Alexander the Great) King Alexander I played a crucial role in maintaining Macedonia's autonomy while navigating the complex power dynamics between the Greek city-states and the Persian Empire. His involvement in the Persian Wars solidified the kingdom's position in the Hellenic world and set the stage for future expansions.

Queen Eurydice I: Queen Eurydice I was instrumental in fostering alliances with neighbouring regions, consolidating the kingdom's power base, and promoting cultural development within the Macedonian court.

SIGNIFICANT PLACES IN ANCIENT MACEDONIA

Aegae (Aigai): Remained the ancient capital of the Macedonian kingdom, Aegae, served as the ceremonial and administrative centre of power for early Macedonian kings. The city was home to the royal palace, where important political and religious ceremonies took place, solidifying the region's cultural and political identity.

Pella: Emerged as the capital under the reign of King Archelaus I, Pella became the vibrant hub of Macedonian political and cultural life. It served as a flourishing centre for art, education, and commerce, showcasing the progressive cultural development and prosperity of ancient Macedonia.

Vergina (Aigai): Continued to be the burial site of many Macedonian kings.

The period following the incorporation of the region into the Roman Republic in 168 B.C. witnessed a significant transformation in the political, cultural, and socio-economic landscape of what is now North Macedonia. Under Roman rule, the region experienced a blending of local traditions with Roman governance, architecture, and culture, leading to the development of a distinct Roman identity within the area.

Following the Roman conquest, North Macedonia became part of the Roman province of Macedonia, which was established in 146 B.C. The region became an essential part of the Roman Empire's strategic and economic interests in the Eastern Mediterranean, serving as a vital crossroads for trade and military routes between Rome and the Eastern territories.

During the Roman period, various cities in the region flourished and developed into significant urban centres, including the prominent city of Stobi (now in modern-day Gradsko). These cities became hubs for trade, commerce, and cultural exchange, fostering the growth of a cosmopolitan society influenced by both Roman and Greek traditions. The construction of roads, bridges, and other infrastructural developments facilitated the integration of the region into the broader Roman Empire.

In the 1st century A.D., the region of Macedonia witnessed the spread of Christianity, with several Christian communities and churches emerging in various cities, contributing to the development of early Christian religious practices and institutions.

Notable figures during this period included the Roman general and statesman Gaius Julius Caesar, who played a crucial role in the Roman Republic's transition into the Roman Empire and who had a significant impact on the political developments in the wider Mediterranean region. Additionally, notable Roman emperors such as Augustus, Tiberius, and Trajan oversaw various administrative and infrastructural projects in the region, contributing to its overall development and integration into the Roman imperial system.

The Roman Conquest and subsequent Roman rule in North Macedonia laid the foundations for the region's continued influence and integration within the broader Roman cultural and political sphere, leaving a lasting legacy that shaped its societal, cultural, and economic dynamics for centuries to come.

In 336 B.C., Philip II of Macedon, known for his ambitious campaigns and political prowess, consolidated his control over Upper Macedonia, encompassing the northern sector and the southern reaches of Paeonia, areas that correspond to the modern-day territory of North Macedonia. This consolidation served as a crucial prelude to the transformative era that followed, setting the stage for the remarkable achievements of his son, Alexander the Great.

Alexander's unparalleled military campaigns resulted in the absorption of a significant portion of the remaining territories into his vast empire, excluding Dardania. This extension of dominion reshaped the geopolitical landscape, leaving an indelible legacy that echoed through generations. His military campaigns and the spread of Hellenistic culture influenced the region's art, architecture, and governance, leaving an enduring mark on the cultural and political identity of the region.

Subsequently, the Romans extended their influence across the broader region, incorporating the majority of the Republic into the province of Macedonia. However, the northern sectors, including Dardania, fell within the boundaries of Moesia, exemplifying the intricate territorial divisions and administrative structures prevalent during this time.

INFLUENTIAL FIGURES DURING MACEDONIAN INTEGRATION INTO THE ROMAN REPUBLIC

Aemilius Paullus: A Roman general known for his victory at the Battle of Pydna in 168 B.C., which marked a significant turning point in the Roman conquest of Macedonia. His military leadership and strategic acumen played a crucial role in the subsequent integration of Macedonia into the Roman Republic.

The Triumph of Aemilius Paulus

Lucius Aemilius Paullus Macedonicus: The son of Aemilius Paullus, he followed in his father's footsteps and played a vital role in the Roman administration of Macedonia after its formal annexation. His governance and diplomatic efforts contributed to the smooth assimilation of Macedonian culture and society into the Roman provincial system.

SIGNIFICANT PLACES DURING THE INTEGRATION OF MACEDONIA INTO THE ROMAN REPUBLIC

Thessalonica (Thessaloniki): A key city in Macedonia, Thessalonica became a prominent hub of Roman influence and culture during the Roman period. It served as an essential administrative centre and a crucial link between Rome and the eastern territories, playing a vital role in the dissemination of Roman governance and cultural assimilation within the region.

Thessalonica Roman Forum

Amphipolis: Positioned strategically along the Strymon River, Amphipolis held great significance as a vital military and commercial centre during the Roman conquest of Macedonia. Its strategic location facilitated Roman control over the region and provided a crucial base for further expansion into the eastern Mediterranean, marking it as a significant landmark in the history of Roman influence in Macedonia.

Amphipolis Fortifications

After the division of the Roman Empire in 395 A.D., the region of North Macedonia fell under the influence of the Byzantine Empire, marking a period of significant cultural, religious, and political change. The Byzantine Empire, with its capital in Constantinople, exerted a profound impact on the region, contributing to the development of a distinct Byzantine cultural and religious identity.

During the early Byzantine period, North Macedonia served as an essential frontier region, facing invasions and migrations of various Slavic tribes from the north. The region became a melting pot of cultural influences, blending the traditions of the indigenous population with those of the incoming Slavic settlers. This period witnessed the emergence of various Slavic tribes, including the South Slavs, who established settlements and communities across the region, shaping its linguistic and cultural landscape.

In the 6th century, South Slavic tribes began to establish settlements within the borders of what is now North Macedonia, ushering in a new era in the region's cultural narrative. Byzantine Greek historians referred to these Slavic settlements as "Sclavenes," who were active participants in various assaults against the Byzantine Empire, either autonomously or in conjunction with the Bulgars or Avars.

The Byzantine Empire, under the rule of influential emperors such as Justinian I, exerted significant efforts to maintain control over the region, undertaking various military campaigns and administrative reforms. Justinian I, known for his ambitious legal and architectural projects, played a crucial role in fortifying the Byzantine presence in North Macedonia and the broader Balkan Peninsula.

The spread of Christianity during the Byzantine period led to the establishment of numerous monasteries, churches, and ecclesiastical institutions across the region.

Monuments such as the resplendent Church of St. Sophia in Ohrid, with its graceful arches and ornate domes that seemed to ascend towards the heavens, and the Basilica of St. Achilleios in the tranquil embrace of Lake Prespa, stood as awe-inspiring testaments to the architectural prowess and spiritual devotion that characterised the Macedonian Byzantine landscape. These monuments, etched with the imprints of Byzantine grandeur, served as sacred spaces that fostered a sense of collective reverence and artistic admiration, nurturing an environment where the divine and the earthly converged in an ensemble of aesthetic brilliance and spiritual contemplation.

Church of St. Sofia in Ohrid

The towering figures of esteemed Byzantine scholars and theologians, such as the revered Clement of Ohrid and the erudite Cyril of Scythopolis, emerged as luminaries of intellectual pursuit and guardians of classical knowledge. Their enduring contributions to the realms of education and the preservation of classical thought fostered an environment where the seeds of intellectual curiosity and scholarly pursuit took root, shaping a legacy of erudition that would continue to reverberate through the corridors of Macedonian thought and culture for centuries to come.

Clement of Ohrid

Notable ecclesiastical figures, including Cyril and Methodius, Byzantine Christian missionaries and brothers, contributed to the dissemination of Christianity and the development of the Glagolitic and Cyrillic alphabets, laying the foundations for the cultural and religious heritage of the Slavic peoples in the region.

Cyril and Methodius Portrait

Around 680, a Bulgar contingent, led by Khan Kuber from the Dulo clan, a lineage shared with the Danubian Bulgarian Khan Asparukh, established their presence in the Pelagonian plain. Subsequently, they launched military campaigns that extended into the region surrounding Thessaloniki, leaving an indelible mark on the geopolitical landscape of the era. The presence of the Bulgars in the region contributed to the evolution of the cultural and political dynamics, leaving lasting imprints on the region's historical narrative.

Towards the conclusion of the 10th century, the landscape of what is now North Macedonia assumed paramount significance within the political and cultural mixture of the First Bulgarian Empire under the rule of the esteemed Tsar Samuel. Concurrently, the Byzantine Emperor Basil II asserted his dominion over the eastern segment of the empire, encompassing the territory of present-day Bulgaria, and assumed control of the then-capital Preslav in 972. This pivotal transition prompted the establishment of a new administrative capital at Ohrid, concurrently serving as the esteemed seat of the Bulgarian Patriarchate. The ascendancy of the Bulgarian model within the broader Slavic cultural milieu ensued, encapsulating a rich legacy that would resonate throughout the annals of history.

INFLUENTIAL FIGURES DURING THE MACEDONIAN BYZANTINE ERA

Clement of Ohrid: A revered Byzantine scholar and theologian, Clement of Ohrid played a pivotal role in the cultural and intellectual flourishing of Macedonia during the Byzantine era. His contributions to education and the preservation of classical knowledge were instrumental in nurturing an environment of intellectual curiosity and scholarly pursuit within the region.

Cyril of Scythopolis: An erudite figure renowned for his scholarly pursuits and theological insights, Cyril of Scythopolis emerged as a beacon of intellectual enlightenment during the Macedonian Byzantine era. His contributions to Byzantine thought and cultural preservation left an indelible mark upon the intellectual landscape of Macedonia, fostering an enduring legacy of erudition and scholarly pursuit.

SIGNIFICANT PLACES DURING THE MACEDONIAN BYZANTINE ERA

Skopje: The historical city of Skopje, nestled along the Vardar River, played a pivotal role in the Byzantine cultural and political landscape of Macedonia. Renowned for its architectural grandeur and cultural vibrancy, Skopje served as a vital centre for the dissemination of Byzantine artistic and intellectual traditions, leaving an indelible imprint upon the cultural fabric of the region during this transformative era.

Ohrid: A prominent city in Macedonia, Ohrid served as a cultural and intellectual hub during the Byzantine era. Renowned for its vibrant artistic heritage and the presence of esteemed scholars and theologians, Ohrid stood as a beacon of creative and intellectual brilliance, nurturing an environment where the realms of art, culture, and scholarship converged to shape a legacy of enduring cultural significance.

Between 1014 and 1371 in North Macedonia's history witnessed the rise and fall of several significant medieval Macedonian empires, marked by a complex interplay of political, cultural, and military developments that shaped the region's identity and historical trajectory.

In 1014 , the First Bulgarian Empire, under the rule of Tsar Samuil, suffered a decisive defeat at the hands of the Byzantine Emperor Basil II in the Battle of Kleidion, leading to the incorporation of the region into the Byzantine Empire. However, the aftermath of this defeat marked the beginning of the rise of the medieval Macedonian Empire, which emerged as a significant political and cultural force in the region.

Following several decades marked by persistent conflicts and tumultuous struggles, Bulgaria eventually fell under Byzantine dominion in 1018, marking a significant shift in the geopolitical dynamics of the region. The entirety of North Macedonia was integrated into the Byzantine Empire as the Theme of Bulgaria, while the prestigious Bulgarian Patriarchate underwent a reduction in status, culminating in its transformation into the Archbishopric of Ohrid. In a notable turn of events, Dobromir Chrysos spearheaded a rebellion against the imperial forces, demonstrating a formidable display of resilience against the Byzantine authority. His resolute stance culminated in an unsuccessful imperial campaign during the autumn of 1197, prompting the emperor to seek a negotiated settlement and acknowledge Dobromir Chrysos's rightful claims to lands stretching between the Strymon and Vardar rivers. This accord solidified his control over key territories, including Strumica and the fortress of Prosek, underscoring the complex interplay of power dynamics and regional authority during this turbulent period in the history of the Balkan Peninsula.

During the unrestrained times of the 13th and 14th centuries, the prevailing Byzantine dominion in the region of modern-day North Macedonia experienced intermittent interludes of Bulgarian and Serbian rule, underscoring the complex interplay of shifting political alliances and regional power dynamics. Notably, Konstantin Asen, a former nobleman hailing from Skopje, ascended to the esteemed position of tsar of Bulgaria, presiding over the realm from 1257 to 1277. Subsequently, Skopje served as a pivotal capital within the Serbian Empire under the influential reign of Stefan Dušan.

Tsar Konstantin Asen

Following the dissolution of the empire, the region fell under the purview of independent local Serbian rulers, chiefly the Mrnjavčević and Dragaš houses, each wielding authority over distinct domains. The city of Prilep emerged as a central locus of power under the rule of the Mrnjavčević house, with notable figures such as King Vukašin Mrnjavčević and his son, King Marko, etching their names into the annals of the region's complex political history. King Marko later aligned himself as a vassal of the Ottoman Empire, ultimately meeting his fate in the fateful Battle of Rovine.

King Marko and King Vukašin Mrnjavčević at Marko's Monastery

The medieval Macedonian Empire, also known as the Second Bulgarian Empire, reached its height under the rule of Tsar Ivan Asen II (1218–1241). Ivan Asen II oversaw a period of remarkable expansion, consolidating control over various territories in the Balkans and establishing strong diplomatic ties with other European powers. His reign witnessed the flourishing of art, literature, and architecture, contributing to the development of a distinct Macedonian cultural identity within the empire. The empire's cultural and religious influence extended to the establishment of numerous monasteries, churches, and cultural institutions, contributing to the preservation and dissemination of the region's rich artistic and religious heritage. However, the decline of the medieval

Macedonian Empire began in the mid-14th century, as it faced internal power struggles and external invasions from the Ottoman Empire, which gradually encroached upon its territories. The Ottoman campaigns, led by influential military leaders such as Murad I and Bayezid I, resulted in the gradual disintegration of the empire and the eventual incorporation of the region into the Ottoman imperial system.

IMPORTANT PLACES DURING THIS ERA

Ohrid: Remained significant as an ecclesiastical centre, Ohrid served as the seat of the Archbishopric of Ohrid, a prestigious religious institution within the Byzantine Empire. The city's rich cultural heritage is reflected in its numerous churches and monasteries, including the iconic Church of St. Sophia and the Church of St. John at Kaneo, which exemplify the region's vibrant architectural and artistic legacy.

Skopje: Growing as a pivotal urban centre, Skopje played a crucial role in the political and cultural dynamics of the medieval Balkans. Its strategic location facilitated its prominence as a hub for trade and commerce, contributing to its reputation as an influential political capital under various ruling entities, including the Second Bulgarian Empire and the Serbian Empire.

Prilep: Prilep was now emerging as a central locus of power during the medieval period, particularly under the reign of the Mrnjavčević house. The city's notable landmarks, including the

Church of St. Nicholas and the Marko's Towers, stand as testaments to its historical and cultural significance within the context of regional power struggles and shifting political alliances.

INFLUENTIAL FIGURES DURING THIS ERA

Tsar Ivan Asen II: Notable for his pivotal role in the consolidation and expansion of the Second Bulgarian Empire, Tsar Ivan Asen II presided over a period of significant territorial growth and diplomatic achievements. His reign witnessed the flourishing of cultural and artistic endeavours, contributing to the establishment of a distinct Macedonian cultural identity within the empire.

King Marko: Recognised for his notable contributions to the complex political landscape of the Balkans, King Marko, the son of King Vukašin Mrnjavčević, emerged as a prominent figure during the tumultuous 14th century. His alignment as a vassal of the Ottoman Empire underscored the intricate power dynamics of the period, ultimately culminating in the fateful Battle of Rovine, which marked a significant turning point in the region's historical trajectory.

From 1371 to 1912 marked a significant era of Ottoman dominance and struggle in the history of North Macedonia, characterised by a complex interplay of political, social, and cultural dynamics that shaped the region's identity and historical trajectory.

Following the gradual disintegration of the medieval Macedonian Empires, North Macedonia fell under the control of the expanding Ottoman Empire. The Ottoman conquest of the region, under the leadership of influential sultans such as Gazi Murad I, Mehmed the Conqueror, and Suleiman the Magnificent, marked the beginning of a prolonged period of Ottoman rule that would last for centuries.

Sultan Gazi Murad I

Simultaneously, during the 12th, 13th, and early 14th centuries, sections of modern western North Macedonia fell under the dominion of the esteemed Albanian Noble Gropa family, who wielded authority over territories stretching from Ohrid to Debar. Following the conclusion of the Gropa rule, the mantle of power was assumed by the influential Albanian Royal House of Kastrioti, which governed the Principality of Kastrioti during the latter half of the 14th century and the initial decades of the 15th century. However, the demise of Albanian Prince Gjon Kastrioti in 1437 marked a turning point, leading to the conquest of numerous territories by the encroaching Ottoman Empire.

Gjergj Kastrioti Skanderbeg

The subsequent resurgence of Albanian authority under the League of Lezhë, spearheaded by Gjergj Kastrioti Skanderbeg, engendered a series of fierce battles across the western territories of modern North Macedonia, with skirmishes like the Battle of Polog, Battle of Mokra, Battle of Ohrid, Battle of Otonetë, Battle of Oranik, and numerous others shaping the regional landscape.

Skanderbeg's valiant campaign into Macedonia bore testament to the fierce resistance put forth by the Albanian forces, yet with his demise in 1468, the once-potent Albanian resistance began to falter. Despite subsequent attempts by Lekë Dukagjini to rejuvenate the Albanian League, the eventual subjugation of the last remaining Albanian strongholds culminated in the Siege of Shkodër in 1479, signifying the waning of Albanian influence within the region and the gradual ascendance of Ottoman authority.

The Ottoman period witnessed the introduction of Islamic culture and institutions, leading to the construction of numerous mosques, madrasas, and other Islamic religious and educational institutions across the region. This period also saw the flourishing of Ottoman art, architecture, and literature, contributing to the development of a rich and diverse cultural heritage that blended elements of both Islamic and Balkan traditions.

However, the Ottoman domination was not without resistance. Throughout the centuries, various uprisings and rebellions emerged in North Macedonia, led by prominent figures such as

Kara Mahmud Bushati and Karposh, who sought to challenge Ottoman authority and reclaim autonomy for the region. These struggles for independence and self-determination underscored the resilience and determination of the local population to resist foreign domination and preserve their cultural and national identity.

The 19th century witnessed the rise of the Ottoman reform movements, such as the Tanzimat and the Young Turks, which aimed to modernise the empire and introduce political and social reforms. These efforts, however, were met with mixed success and faced challenges as the empire grappled with internal strife and external pressures from European powers, leading to the gradual decline of Ottoman influence in the region.

The valley of the Vardar River, which would later emerge as the central region of North Macedonia, remained under Ottoman rule prior to the First Balkan War of 1912, with a brief interlude in 1878 when it was liberated from Ottoman control following the Russo-Turkish War, subsequently joining the domain of Bulgaria. Notably, the year 1903 witnessed the proclamation of the short-lived Kruševo Republic in the southwestern part of present-day North Macedonia, founded by the insurgents of the Ilinden–Preobrazhenie Uprising, underscoring the fervent spirit of resistance against the prevailing Ottoman authority.

Throughout the span of Ottoman rule, numerous ethnographers and travellers often categorised the Slavic-speaking populace in Macedonia as Bulgarians, a trend exemplified by figures such as the 17th-century traveller Evliya Çelebi in his Seyahatname, as well as the Ottoman census conducted by Hilmi Pasha in 1904 and subsequent years. However, observations also acknowledged the distinct linguistic character of the region, often characterised as a "Western Bulgarian dialect" akin to other Bulgarian dialects in modern western Bulgaria.

Additionally, historical evidence indicates a fluidity in the ethnic identity of certain Macedonian Slavs, with some identifying as Serbs, particularly in the northern regions, while a pronounced inclination towards joining Greece prevailed in southern Macedonia, garnering support from a substantial segment of the Slavic-speaking populace. Scholars suggest that the understanding of ethnicity during medieval times was markedly more fluid than contemporary conceptions, influenced by the nineteenth-century rise of nationalistic ideals aligned with the concept of a homogeneous nation-state.

INFLUENTIAL FIGURES DURING THE OTTOMAN DOMINION IN MACEDONIA

Yunus Nadi Bey: A prominent Ottoman military commander, Yunus Bey played a significant role in the governance and administration of Macedonia during the Ottoman dominion. His efforts in consolidating Ottoman rule and maintaining regional stability left an indelible mark upon the political landscape of the region.

Yunus Nadi Bey

Ali Pasha of Ohrid: Notable for his political prowess and diplomatic finesse, Ali Pasha of Ohrid emerged as a key figure in the socio-political affairs of Macedonia during the Ottoman era. His contributions to the cultural and administrative spheres of the region served to foster a sense of unity and cooperation among the diverse communities that inhabited the land.

Atik Ali Pasha Mosque

SIGNIFICANT PLACES DURING THE OTTOMAN DOMINION IN MACEDONIA

Bitola: A vital cultural and economic hub during the Ottoman dominion, Bitola served as a crucial center for trade and cultural exchange within the region. Renowned for its bustling bazaars and architectural grandeur, Bitola stood as a testament to the enduring legacy of Ottoman influence upon the socio-cultural elements of Macedonia during this era.

Skopje: As a historical city of immense cultural and political significance, Skopje played a pivotal role in the governance and administration of Macedonia under Ottoman rule. Renowned for its diverse communities and vibrant cultural landscape, Skopje served as a beacon of socio-political dynamism and intercultural exchange within the Ottoman domain, leaving an indelible imprint upon the historical fabric of the region.

The period from 1912 to 1913 marked a crucial juncture in the history of North Macedonia, characterised by the Balkan Wars and the subsequent process of Macedonian unification. During this period, the region witnessed a series of conflicts and diplomatic maneuvers that would ultimately shape its political and territorial landscape.

The Balkan Wars, which occurred between 1912 and 1913, were a series of military conflicts between the Balkan states, including Bulgaria, Greece, Montenegro, and Serbia, on one side, and the Ottoman Empire on the other. These wars aimed to liberate various territories under Ottoman rule and establish the national sovereignty of the Balkan states.

During the First Balkan War (1912), the Balkan League, comprising Bulgaria, Greece, Montenegro, and Serbia, launched a successful campaign against the Ottoman Empire, leading to the capture of significant territories in the Balkans, including parts of North Macedonia. The Treaty of London (1913) sought to redefine the territorial boundaries in the Balkans, leading to a redistribution of the region's political and geographical landscape.

The region was captured by the Kingdom of Serbia during the First Balkan War of 1912 and was subsequently annexed to Serbia under the Karađorđević dynasty in the post-war peace treaties except the Strumica region, which was part of Bulgaria between 1912 and 1919. It had no administrative autonomy and was called South Serbia (Južna Srbija) or "Old Serbia" (Stara Srbija). It was occupied by the Kingdom of Bulgaria between 1915 and 1918. After the First World War, the Kingdom of Serbia joined the newly formed Kingdom of Serbs, Croats and Slovenes.

London Peace Treaty Signing 30 May 1913

The Second Balkan War (1913) ensued shortly after the First Balkan War, as tensions escalated among the Balkan states over territorial disputes and the division of captured territories. The conflict resulted in a reconfiguration of territorial control and power dynamics in the region, leading to the establishment of new political boundaries and the emergence of a redefined geopolitical landscape in the Balkans.

The Macedonian unification movement, led by influential figures such as Goce Delchev, Dame Gruev, and Nikola Karev, aimed to secure the territorial integrity and political autonomy of the Macedonian region. Their efforts, rooted in the aspirations for a unified and independent Macedonian state, laid the groundwork for the subsequent developments and negotiations that would shape the region's political and national identity in the years to come.

The period from 1912 to 1913 , marked by the Balkan Wars and the Macedonian unification movement, played a pivotal role in defining the contemporary political and territorial boundaries of North Macedonia, setting the stage for its subsequent nation-building efforts and the establishment of a distinct national identity within the broader context of the Balkans. The Karađorđević period, spanning from 1912 to 1944, signified a crucial phase in the historical evolution of the Balkan Peninsula, marked by a series of transformative events and significant socio-political shifts that left an enduring imprint on the region's cultural and geopolitical landscape.

IMPORTANT PLACES DURING THIS TIME:

Skopje: Serving as a significant urban centre during the early 20th century, Skopje played a vital role in the unfolding political and territorial developments in the region. Its strategic location and historical significance contributed to its prominence as a focal point for diplomatic negotiations and administrative activities, reflecting its enduring importance within the context of the Balkan Wars and the subsequent process of Macedonian unification.

Bitola: Known for its historical and cultural heritage, Bitola served as an essential hub for various political and administrative functions during the early 20th century. Its strategic location facilitated its role as a vital communication and trade centre, contributing to its prominence within the broader context of regional political manoeuvres and territorial reconfigurations.

INFLUENTIAL FIGURES DURING THIS TIME:

Nikola Karev: Notable for his active involvement in the Macedonian liberation movement, Nikola Karev played a crucial role in advocating for the territorial integrity and political autonomy of the Macedonian region during the early 20th century. His dedication to the advancement of Macedonian national interests and his contributions to the pursuit of an independent Macedonian state underscored his significance as a key figure in the historical narrative of North Macedonia during this transformative period.

Nikola Karev

Goce Delchev: Renowned for his pivotal role in the Macedonian revolutionary movement, Goce Delchev emerged as a prominent figure during the early 20th century. His unwavering commitment to the Macedonian cause and his efforts to promote the ideals of Macedonian autonomy and unification left a lasting impact on the region's political and national consciousness, cementing his status as an influential figure in the struggle for Macedonian independence.

Goce Delchev

The interwar period and World War II, spanning from 1919 to 1945 , marked a tumultuous and transformative era in the history of North Macedonia, characterised by political upheavals, territorial reconfigurations, and the devastating impact of global conflict on the region.

Following the conclusion of World War I, the Treaty of Versailles in 1919 redefined the political landscape of Europe, leading to the dissolution of various empires and the establishment of new nation-states. The Kingdom of Serbs, Croats, and Slovenes (later known as Yugoslavia) was created, incorporating the region of Vardar Macedonia, which encompassed the present-day territory of North Macedonia.

During the interwar period, Vardar Macedonia experienced significant political and social changes within the framework of the newly established Kingdom of Yugoslavia. The region witnessed efforts to consolidate its national identity and cultural heritage, while grappling with political and economic challenges within the broader Yugoslav state.

The rise of fascism in Europe and the onset of World War II in 1939 had profound implications for North Macedonia. The region faced the devastating impact of the war, including military occupation, political repression, and widespread socio-economic disruptions. The Axis powers, particularly Nazi Germany and Fascist Italy, exerted control over the region, imposing their totalitarian ideologies and policies that led to widespread suffering and resistance among the local population.

During World War II, the Macedonian population actively participated in the resistance movements against the Axis occupation. The anti-fascist resistance movement, led by figures such as Metodija Andonov-Čento and Panko Brashnarov, played a crucial role in organizing partisan resistance and liberation efforts, contributing to the broader struggle for the liberation of Yugoslavia from Axis control.

Metodija Andonov-Čento

The end of World War II in 1945 marked a significant turning point in the region's history, as the establishment of the Socialist Federal Republic of Yugoslavia led to the reconfiguration of political and social structures, shaping the trajectory of North Macedonia's development within the framework of the Yugoslav federation. The Vardar Banovina, a historically significant region, endured a period of occupation from 1941 to 1944 by two distinct Axis powers, specifically Italian-ruled Albania and pro-German Bulgaria, each asserting their dominion over different segments of the territory.

Amidst the tumult of occupation, the inhabitants of the Vardar Banovina who resisted the oppressive regimes faced persecution and reprisals, compelling some to align themselves with the Communist resistance movement led by Josip Broz Tito. The emergence of the Communist resistance movement represented a pivotal chapter in the region's history, reflecting the steadfast determination of the local populace to resist the forces of oppression and occupation. This movement fostered a spirit of collective defiance and resilience against the encroaching Axis powers.

Notably, the Bulgarian army's entry into Macedonia was met with a relatively favourable reception by a significant portion of the local population, and the Bulgarian forces were able to enlist substantial support from the indigenous communities. Reports indicate that as much as 40% to 60% of the soldiers in certain battalions were drawn from the local Macedonian populace, underscoring the nuanced complexities and varying allegiances that characterised the regional response to the occupation forces during the tumultuous years of World War II.

The period from 1919 to 1945, encompassing the interwar period and World War II, left a profound and lasting impact on North Macedonia's socio-political and cultural landscape, shaping its historical trajectory and contributing to the broader narrative of resistance and resilience within the Balkan region.

IMPORTANT PLACES DURING THIS ERA:

Skopje: Despite facing significant destruction during World War II, Skopje remained a vital urban centre with historical and cultural significance throughout the interwar period and the war. Its strategic location and role as a regional administrative hub underscored its enduring importance within the broader context of political and social developments in North Macedonia.

Bitola: Recognised for its rich cultural heritage and historical significance, Bitola maintained its prominence as an important cultural and administrative centre during the interwar period and World War II. Its historical landmarks and strategic location contributed to its continued significance within the context of the region's socio-political and military dynamics.

INFLUENTIAL FIGURES DURING THIS ERA:

Panko Brashnarov: Recognised for his active involvement in the anti-fascist resistance movement, Panko Brashnarov contributed to the organised efforts of the partisan forces in North Macedonia during World War II. His dedication to the resistance movement and his role in mobilizing local communities against the occupying Axis powers reflected the spirit of resilience and defiance that defined the region's struggle for liberation and independence.

Panko Brashnarov

Metodija Andonov-Čento: Noted for his leadership in the anti-fascist resistance movement, Metodija Andonov-Čento emerged as a prominent figure during World War II, playing a crucial role in organizing and coordinating partisan resistance efforts against the Axis occupation. His commitment to the liberation of Yugoslavia from fascist control exemplified his significant contribution to the region's history during this tumultuous period.

During 1945 to 1991 marked the socialist era in the history of North Macedonia, characterised by the region's integration into the Socialist Federal Republic of Yugoslavia under the leadership of Josip Broz Tito. This period witnessed significant social, political, and economic transformations that shaped the trajectory of North Macedonia's development within the broader Yugoslav federation.

Josip Broz Tito

Following the end of World War II, North Macedonia became an integral part of the newly established Socialist Federal Republic of Yugoslavia, which sought to foster a unified socialist state built on the principles of self-management and non-alignment. The Yugoslav government, under Tito's leadership, implemented various social and economic reforms aimed at modernising the country and improving the living standards of its citizens.

The socialist era witnessed the rapid industrialisation and urbanisation of North Macedonia, as the region became a key industrial and economic hub within the Yugoslav federation. The development of industries, such as metallurgy, textiles, and chemicals, contributed to the region's economic growth and fostered the expansion of its urban centres, including Skopje, Bitola, and Kumanovo.

The period also saw significant investments in education, healthcare, and infrastructure, as the Yugoslav government prioritised the development of human capital and social welfare programs. The establishment of educational institutions and cultural organisations aimed to promote the region's cultural heritage and linguistic identity within the framework of the broader Yugoslav multinational and multilingual state.

The socialist era, while marked by relative stability and economic progress, was not without its challenges. Diverging national interests and economic disparities within the Yugoslav federation led to political and social frictions among the constituent republics, ultimately contributing to the dissolution of Yugoslavia and the outbreak of ethnic conflicts in the 1990s.

The eventual disintegration of the Socialist Federal Republic of Yugoslavia in the early 1990s led to the declaration of independence by several republics, including the Republic of Macedonia. This marked the beginning of a new chapter in the history of the region, accompanied by a series of political and social challenges that would shape the trajectory of the newly independent nation in the years to come.

In the quest for sovereignty, the Republic of Macedonia underwent significant transitions from a socialist state to a parliamentary democracy. Multi-party elections in 1990 marked the onset of a new era of political pluralism and democratic governance within the country. Constitutional amendments and parliamentary resolutions paved the way for the nation's journey towards full-fledged independence.

A significant milestone was reached with the conduct of an independence referendum in 1991, wherein an overwhelming majority voted in favour of seceding from the Yugoslav federation and establishing the Republic of Macedonia as an independent sovereign state. The adoption of the Declaration of Independence and a new Constitution solidified the nation's commitment to democratic governance and constitutional adherence, marking pivotal milestones in the consolidation of the country's newfound independence and statehood.

Kumanovo: During the socialist era, Kumanovo experienced significant industrial development and urban expansion, emerging as a key industrial centre within North Macedonia. Its strategic location and growing industrial sector contributed to its prominence as an important economic hub within the broader Yugoslav federation, reflecting the region's socio-economic transformation during this period.

Bitola: Despite its historical significance, Bitola continued to thrive as a cultural and educational centre during the socialist era. Its educational institutions and cultural organisations played a crucial role in preserving and promoting the region's cultural heritage and linguistic identity within the context of the Yugoslav multinational state, underscoring its continued importance as a centre of cultural and intellectual activity.

INFLUENTIAL FIGURES DURING THIS ERA:

Lazar Koliševski: Noted for his prominent role within the Yugoslav Communist Party and the political leadership of North Macedonia, Lazar Koliševski played a crucial part in shaping the region's socialist development during the post-World War II era. His contributions to the implementation of social and economic reforms, as well as his involvement in the promotion of socialist ideals and principles, underscored his significance as a key figure in the history of North Macedonia during this transformative period.

Krste Crvenkovski: Recognised for his active involvement in the political and social developments of North Macedonia during the socialist era, Krste Crvenkovski contributed to the region's political landscape as a prominent figure within the Yugoslav political framework. His role in advocating for regional interests and fostering the region's socio-economic progress reflected his influence in shaping the trajectory of North Macedonia's development within the broader Yugoslav federation.

Krste Crvenkovski

1991 to 1995 marked a critical phase in the history of North Macedonia, characterised by the country's declaration of independence from the Socialist Federal Republic of Yugoslavia and the subsequent efforts to establish its identity as a sovereign nation within the international community.

On September 8, 1991, the Republic of North Macedonia declared its independence from Yugoslavia following a referendum in which the majority of the population voted in favour of secession. This marked a significant milestone in the country's history, as it embarked on a path toward establishing itself as an independent and sovereign state.

The early years of independence were marked by various political and economic challenges as the newly formed state grappled with the process of nation-building and the establishment of democratic institutions. The government, led by the first President Kiro Gligorov, and the first Prime Minister Nikola Kljusev, focused on fostering stability, promoting economic development, and establishing diplomatic relations with other countries in the region and the broader international community.

During this period, North Macedonia faced significant challenges related to its internal political dynamics and its external relations with neighbouring countries, particularly with regards to the resolution of territorial disputes and the establishment of bilateral relations. The country actively pursued diplomatic efforts to establish peaceful relations and engage in regional cooperation initiatives, contributing to the broader efforts of promoting stability and security in the Balkans.

The early years of independence also witnessed the establishment of key democratic institutions, including the formation of a multi-party system, the development of a new constitution, and the implementation of political and economic reforms aimed at fostering a free-market economy and promoting the rule of law.

The international recognition of the Republic of North Macedonia as an independent state by the United Nations and other international organisations further solidified its position within the global community, laying the foundations for its continued participation in regional and international affairs.

Following the disintegration of Yugoslavia, the early years of the newly formed Macedonian republic were marked by considerable uncertainty regarding the status of ethnic Albanians within the country. This period saw the emergence of various Albanian political parties, most notably the Party for Democratic Prosperity (PDP), which spearheaded efforts to secure improved rights for Albanians in North Macedonia. The PDP advocated for a range of measures, including expanded educational rights, the promotion of the Albanian language, constitutional reforms, the release of political prisoners, the implementation of a proportional voting system, and an end to discriminatory practices.

Tensions escalated as the PDP leader, Nevzat Halili, declared the party's intention to disregard the constitution and pursue autonomy. In 1992 and again in 2014, Halili declared the establishment of the Republic of Ilirida, a move that was promptly deemed unconstitutional by the Macedonian government, further exacerbating the already volatile political climate.

Nevzat Halili

The international recognition of the newly formed Macedonian state encountered significant hurdles, primarily stemming from Greece's objection to the country's chosen name and national symbols, precipitating the infamous Macedonia naming dispute. While Bulgaria swiftly extended recognition to the Republic of Macedonia, Greece's objection led to a delay in international recognition, culminating in the country's admission to the United Nations under the provisional name of "the former Yugoslav Republic of Macedonia" on 8 April 1993.

Greece's dissatisfaction ultimately culminated in a trade blockade imposed in February 1994, which was subsequently lifted in September 1995 after Macedonia made certain concessions, including amendments to its flag and constitutional provisions perceived as impinging on the sovereignty of neighbouring states. The normalisation of relations between the two countries followed, but the naming dispute continued to be a contentious issue, drawing sharp divisions within local and international political circles.

IMPORTANT PLACES DURING THIS ERA:

Skopje: As the capital and largest city of North Macedonia, Skopje served as the focal point for the country's political, economic, and cultural activities during the early years of independence. Its strategic significance as a major urban centre contributed to its prominence as a hub for diplomatic negotiations, administrative functions, and socio-cultural development within the newly established republic.

Ohrid: Noted for its historical and cultural significance, Ohrid played a pivotal role in preserving the country's rich heritage and fostering its cultural identity within the international community. The city's renowned landmarks, including the Ohrid Lake and the Church of St. Sophia, served as symbols of the nation's historical legacy and contributed to the promotion of North Macedonia's cultural heritage and tourism industry.

Kiro Gligorov: Notable for his pivotal role as the first President of the Republic of Macedonia, Kiro Gligorov played a significant part in guiding the country through the crucial early years of independence. His leadership in fostering stability, promoting democratic values, and pursuing diplomatic initiatives within the region and the international community underscored his influence in shaping the trajectory of North Macedonia's development as a sovereign nation during this transformative period.

Kiro Gligorov

61

Nikola Kljusev: Recognised for his contributions as the first Prime Minister of the Republic of Macedonia, Nikola Kljusev played a key role in implementing political and economic reforms aimed at fostering a free-market economy and promoting democratic governance within the country. His efforts in establishing diplomatic relations with neighbouring countries and engaging in regional cooperation initiatives reflected his influence in shaping the country's political and diplomatic landscape during the critical years following independence.

Nikola Kljusev

From 1995 to 2001 marked a crucial phase in the history of North Macedonia, considered by the country's continued efforts to consolidate its democratic institutions, foster political stability, and address various challenges related to nation-building and socio-economic development.

North Macedonia faced a series of challenges, including the consolidation of democratic institutions, the promotion of inter-ethnic harmony, and the implementation of economic reforms aimed at fostering sustainable development and integration into the broader European community.

War in Kosovo – 1999

The Kosovo War in 1999 precipitated a significant humanitarian crisis, with approximately 340,000 Albanian refugees from Kosovo seeking shelter in the Republic of Macedonia, straining the delicate equilibrium between the Macedonian and Albanian communities. The influx of refugees disrupted the region's normalcy, necessitating the establishment of refugee camps within the country.

During this period, Athens refrained from interfering with the Republic's affairs, facilitating the passage of NATO forces through the region en route to potential military intervention in the Federal Republic of Yugoslavia. Thessaloniki emerged as a pivotal hub for the distribution of humanitarian aid to the affected regions, underscoring the regional cooperation in the face of the humanitarian crisis.

While the agreement between Yugoslav President Slobodan Milošević and NATO facilitated the return of refugees under UN protection, the Kosovo War engendered heightened tensions between the Macedonian and Albanian communities, straining inter-ethnic relations within the country. Despite the challenges, the coordinated stance of Athens and Ankara in advocating a position of non-involvement offered a semblance of regional stability, even as Greece experienced significant domestic opposition to NATO and the USA in the aftermath of the conflict.

Amidst these efforts, the nation faced internal challenges, notably the emergence of the National Liberation Army (NLA), an ethnic Albanian insurgent group in the northern and northwestern regions of the country. The NLA advocated for constitutional reforms to safeguard the rights of the Albanian minority, leading to significant geopolitical tensions.

During the spring of 2001, the NLA, emerged in the northern and northwestern regions of the Republic of Macedonia, advocating for constitutional reforms to protect the rights of the Albanian minority, particularly concerning language rights. The NLA garnered support from Albanian communities in NATO-controlled Kosovo and Albanian guerrillas positioned in the demilitarised zone between Kosovo and the remaining parts of Serbia. Subsequently, in June 2001, following a joint crackdown by NATO and Serbian forces and subsequent negotiations overseen by EU officials, the NLA agreed to a ceasefire.

However, in August 2001, the successful "Operations Essential Harvest," involving 3,500 NATO soldiers retrieving arms, culminated in the formal disbandment of the NLA in September, fostering a sense of peace and stability within the country.

Key events during this period include the signing of the Ohrid Framework Agreement in 2001, which aimed to address the ethnic tensions and conflicts within the country and promote greater inclusion and representation of the ethnic Albanian minority in the political and social spheres. The agreement facilitated the devolution of political power and the recognition of the Albanian language as an official language in areas with a significant Albanian population, contributing to the promotion of ethnic harmony and political stability within the country.

Ohrid Framework Agreement Signing 13 Aug 2001

The period also witnessed the continued engagement of North Macedonia with the international community and its efforts to promote regional cooperation and integration. The country actively participated in various regional initiatives and diplomatic efforts aimed at fostering stability and cooperation in the Balkans, contributing to the broader efforts of promoting peace and security in the region.

Important political figures during this period included President Boris Trajkovski and Prime Minister Ljubco Georgievski, who played key roles in promoting political stability, fostering inter-ethnic dialogue, and implementing democratic reforms aimed at strengthening the rule of law and promoting social cohesion within the country.

The government's efforts to implement economic reforms, attract foreign investment, and promote sustainable development also played a crucial role in fostering economic growth and improving the standard of living for the country's citizens. These initiatives contributed to the gradual integration of North Macedonia into the broader European community and its ongoing aspirations for European Union membership.

IMPORTANT PLACES DURING THIS ERA:

Tetovo: Noted for its historical and cultural significance, Tetovo served as an important urban centre with a significant Albanian population during the period from 1995 to 2001. The city's strategic location and cultural diversity underscored its importance as a hub for inter-ethnic dialogue and cooperation, reflecting its pivotal role in fostering social cohesion and harmony within the country.

The City of Tetovo

Kumanovo: Recognised for its economic and industrial significance, Kumanovo played a crucial role in the country's economic development and integration into the broader European community during the period from 1995 to 2001. Its strategic location and growing industrial sector contributed to its prominence as a key economic hub within North Macedonia, reflecting the region's ongoing efforts to foster sustainable development and attract foreign investment.

INFLUENTIAL FIGURES DURING THIS ERA:

Boris Trajkovski: Noted for his significant role as the President of North Macedonia during the late 1990s and early 2000s, Boris Trajkovski played a crucial part in promoting political stability, fostering inter-ethnic dialogue, and implementing democratic reforms aimed at strengthening the rule of law and promoting social cohesion within the country. His efforts in engaging with the international community and promoting regional cooperation underscored his influence in shaping the trajectory of North Macedonia's development during this transformative period.

President Boris Trajkovski

Ljubčo Georgievski: Recognised for his contributions as the Prime Minister of North Macedonia during the late 1990s and early 2000s, Ljubčo Georgievski played a key role in implementing economic reforms, attracting foreign investment, and promoting sustainable development within the country. His efforts in fostering economic growth and promoting the country's integration into the European community reflected his influence in shaping the country's socio-economic landscape during the critical years of nation-building and development.

Ljubco Georgievski

The period from 2001 to 2023 marked a significant era in the history of North Macedonia, characterised by the country's persistent efforts towards European integration, socio-economic development, and political stability. During this time, North Macedonia underwent a series of transformative developments that solidified its position within the broader European community and shaped its contemporary political and social landscape.

The Ohrid Framework Agreement was a pivotal milestone, representing an essential step towards addressing inter-ethnic tensions and promoting greater inclusion of the Albanian minority. This agreement laid the foundation for a more stable and inclusive political environment, fostering greater inter-ethnic cooperation and representation within the government.

In June 2017, the political landscape of North Macedonia witnessed a significant shift as of the Social Democratic Union of Macedonia (SDSM) assumed the role of Prime Minister after early elections, bringing an end to an 11-year rule under the conservative VMRO-DPMNE led by former Prime Minister Nikola Gruevski.

The geopolitical scenario experienced a momentous turn in June 2018 with the signing of the Prespa Agreement between the governments of Greece and the Republic of Macedonia. This landmark agreement paved the way for the renaming of the Republic of Macedonia to the Republic of North Macedonia, resolving longstanding disputes and fostering improved diplomatic relations.

In the wake of these developments, May 2019 marked the inauguration of Stevo Pendarovski of the SDSM as the new President of North Macedonia. Subsequently, the nation underwent early parliamentary elections on 15 July 2020, leading to the reinstatement of Zoran Zaev as the Prime Minister of the Republic of North Macedonia in August 2020.

Nevertheless, the political landscape experienced further shifts as Prime Minister Zaev resigned following the SDSM's losses in local elections in October 2021. Internal party leadership elections resulted in Dimitar Kovačevski assuming leadership of the SDSM on 12 December 2021, subsequently being sworn in as the new Prime Minister of North Macedonia on 16 January 2022, leading a new SDSM-led coalition cabinet and illustrating the evolving dynamics within the country's political realm.

The period from 2001 to 2023, characterised by North Macedonia's unwavering commitment to European integration, socio-economic progress, and regional stability, played a critical role in shaping the country's contemporary political, economic, and social landscape, laying a solid foundation for its continued integration into the European community and its aspirations for a prosperous and peaceful future.

Skopje: Serving as the capital and largest city of North Macedonia, Skopje has been a crucial political, economic, and cultural centre throughout the period. It has played a significant role in the country's development and has been a focal point for various political, economic, and cultural activities. Skopje's strategic importance has made it a symbol of the nation's progress and aspirations for integration into the broader European community.

Ohrid: Ohrid plays an increasingly vital role in preserving the country's rich heritage and fostering its cultural identity within the international community. The city's renowned landmarks, including the Ohrid Lake and the Church of St. Sophia, have served as symbols of the nation's historical legacy and have contributed to the promotion of North Macedonia's cultural heritage and tourism industry.

Tetovo: Tetovo has developed into an important urban centre with a significant Albanian population during the period. Its strategic location and cultural diversity have highlighted its role as a hub for inter-ethnic dialogue and cooperation, reflecting its pivotal role in fostering social cohesion and harmony within the country.

Kumanovo: Kumanovo has increasingly played a crucial role in the country's economic development and integration into the broader European community. Its strategic location and growing industrial sector have contributed to its prominence as a key economic hub within North Macedonia, reflecting the region's ongoing efforts to foster sustainable development and attract foreign investment.

INFLUENTIAL FIGURES DURING THIS ERA:

Zoran Zaev: Noted for his significant role as the Prime Minister of North Macedonia, particularly from 2017 to 2021, Zoran Zaev played a crucial part in advancing the country's European integration agenda, fostering political stability, and promoting socio-economic development. His leadership in navigating complex political landscapes and fostering diplomatic relations, notably with the signing of the Prespa Agreement in 2018, underscored his influence in shaping the country's contemporary political and diplomatic trajectory during this transformative period.

Zoran Zaev

Stevo Pendarovski: Recognised for his contributions as the President of North Macedonia from May 2019 onwards, Stevo Pendarovski played a key role in promoting national unity, fostering inter-ethnic harmony, and representing the country in the international arena. His efforts in advocating for stability, inclusivity, and diplomatic engagement have underscored his influence in shaping North Macedonia's position within the global community and in advancing the nation's aspirations for European integration and socio-political progress.

Stevo Pendarovski

Name	Periods
Metodija Andonov – Čento	1991 – 1999
Boris Trajkovski	1999 – 2004
Branko Crvenkovski	2004 – 2009
Gjorge Ivanov	2009 – 2019
Stevo Pendarovski	2019 – 2020
Zoran Zaev	2020 – 2021
Dimitar Kovačevski	2022 – to date

Alexander the Great (356–323 B.C.) - Ancient Macedonian king, known for his military conquests.

Philip II of Macedon (382–336 B.C.) - Father of Alexander the Great, known for expanding the Macedonian kingdom.

Cyril and Methodius (9th century) - Byzantine Christian theologians and missionaries, creators of the Glagolitic and Cyrillic alphabets.

Samuel of Bulgaria (958–1014) - Tsar of the First Bulgarian Empire, ruling over a significant part of the Balkans, including Macedonia.

Justin I (450–527) - Byzantine Emperor who reigned during a critical period of transition for the Eastern Roman Empire, which included parts of Macedonia.

Justinian I (482–565) - Byzantine Emperor known for his significant legal reforms and expansion of the Byzantine Empire into the West, including parts of Macedonia.

Tsar Samuil (c. 958–1014) - Ruler of the First Bulgarian Empire, known for his resistance against the Byzantine Empire.

Kuzman Josifoski Pitu (1879–1944) - Macedonian revolutionary and activist for the rights of the Macedonian people.

Goce Delčev (1872–1903) - Macedonian revolutionary and national hero known for his role in the fight for Macedonian independence.

Dimitar Vlahov (1872–1953) - Prominent political and cultural figure in the development of the Macedonian nation.

Metodija Andonov - Čento (1924–2014) - Founding member of the Macedonian Academy of Sciences and Arts and a prominent political figure.

Kiro Gligorov (1917–2012) - First President of the Republic of Macedonia, played a crucial role in the country's independence.

Ljubčo Georgievski (1966–) - Former Prime Minister of the Republic of Macedonia, known for his political contributions.

Branko Crvenkovski (1962–) - Former President and Prime Minister of the Republic of Macedonia, known for his role in the country's political development.

Boris Trajkovski (1956–2004) - Former President of the Republic of Macedonia, played a crucial role in the peace negotiations during the 2001 insurgency.

Gjorge Ivanov (1960–) - Former President of the Republic of Macedonia, known for his contributions to the country's political stability.

Nikola Gruevski (1970–) - Former Prime Minister of the Republic of Macedonia, known for his economic and political reforms.

Zoran Zaev (1974–) - Current Prime Minister of North Macedonia, known for his efforts in the resolution of the long-standing name dispute with Greece.

Stevo Pendarovski (1963–) - Current President of North Macedonia, known for his diplomatic efforts and contributions to the country's stability.

Dimitar Dimov (1909–1966) - Renowned Macedonian novelist and playwright, known for his significant contributions to Macedonian literature.

This list comprises figures from various fields who have played important roles in shaping the history, culture, and politics of Macedonia.

INDEX

Titles	Citations
Macedonian Coat of Arms	Public domain, via Wikimedia Commons
The Emblem of North Macedonia	MacedonianBoy, Public domain, via Wikimedia Commons
Map of Macedonia	TUBS, CC BY-SA 3.0, via Wikimedia Commons
Ancient City of Pella	Holger Uwe Schmitt, CC BY-SA 4.0, via Wikimedia Commons
Tomb of Philip II in Vergina	Explorer1940, CC BY-SA 4.0, via Wikimedia Commons
Twelve Gods of Olympus	Walters Art Museum, Public domain, via Wikimedia Commons
King Philip II	Richard Mortel, CC BY 2.0, via Wikimedia Commons
King Alexander I (Alexander the Great)	Acropolis Museum, CC BY-SA 2.5, via Wikimedia Commons
The Triumph of Aemilius Paulus	Carle Vernet, Public domain, via Wikimedia Commons
Thessaloniki Roman Forum	Evilemperorzorg at English Wikipedia, CC BY-SA 3.0, via Wikimedia Commons
Amphipolis Fortifications	Marsyas assumed, CC BY-SA 3.0, via Wikimedia Commons
Church of St. Sofia in Ohrid	Petar Milošević, CC BY-SA 4.0, via Wikimedia Commons
Clement of Ohrid	Yane Bakreski, CC BY-SA 4.0, via Wikimedia Commons
Cyril and Methodius Portrait	Nonoumasy, CC BY-SA 4.0, via Wikimedia Commons
Tsar Konstantine Asen	Bichoes78, CC BY-SA 4.0, via Wikimedia Commons
King Marko and King Vukašin Mrnjavčević	ГП, CC BY-SA, via Wikimedia Commons
Sultan Gazi Murad I	Belli Değil Public domain, via Wikimedia Commons
Gjergj Kastrioti Skanderbeg	Public domain, via Wikimedia Commons
Yunus Nadi Bey	Public domain, via Wikimedia Commons
Atik Ali Pasha Mosque	Dosseman, CC BY-SA, via Wikimedia Commons
London Peace Treaty Signing 30 May 1913	Public domain, via Wikimedia Commons
Goce Delchev	Aleksandar Vladikov, Public domain, via Wikimedia Commons
Nikola Karev	Public domain, via Wikimedia Commons
Metodija Andonov-Čento	Public domain, via Wikimedia Commons
Panko Brashnarov	Public domain, via Wikimedia Commons
Josip Broz Tito	Public domain, via Wikimedia Commons
Krste Crvenkovski	Public domain, via Wikimedia Commons
Kiro Gligorov	European Commission, Attribution, via Wikimedia Commons
Nikola Kljusev	Public domain, via Wikimedia Commons
Nevzat Halili	See page for author, CC BY-SA 4.0, via Wikimedia Commons
Ohrid Framework Agreement Signing 13 Aug 2001	CC BY-SA 4.0, via Wikimedia Commons
War in Kosovo - 1999	Kevin Capon, CC BY-SA 3.0, via Wikimedia Commons
The City of Tetovo	Ggia, CC BY-SA 3.0, via Wikimedia Commons
Ljubco Georgievski	Konstantin Pavlov, CC BY-SA 3.0, via Wikimedia Commons
Zoran Zaev	Vlada.mk, CC BY-SA 4.0, via Wikimedia Commons
Stevo Pendarovski	Christophe Licoppe / European Commission, Attribution, via Wikimedia Commons

ABOUT THE AUTHOR

Martin Miller-Yianni, a London native born in 1958, emerged from a humble working-class background. Despite starting his career as a primary school teacher, an unexpected turn of events led him to venture into Southeastern Europe in 2005. Since then, Martin has fully embraced the unique way of life and culture of the region, igniting a passion for writing within him. Having served as a journalist and researcher for a leading information website about this area, he has developed a profound knowledge, understanding, and first-hand experience of this part of the world. Martin's intimate connection with Southeastern Europe, rooted in both personal and professional experiences, continues to inspire and influence his literary pursuits. His latest literary work on Macedonia is a testament to his deep appreciation and admiration for the region's rich and captivating heritage.

365 Bulgarian Adventures (2006)
Publication
Pending

26 Tales of Humanities Trials (2023)
ISBN
978-619-92494-8-2

Simple Treasures in Bulgaria (2008)
ISBN
978-0-9559-8490-7

I'm Bad at Poems (2022)
ISBN
978-619-92494-2-0

Bulgaria Through the Ages (2023)
ISBN
978-1-4476-2777-7

Redemption of Love (2023)
ISBN
978-619-92494-0-6

100 Essential Recipes from Bulgaria (2011)
ISBN
978-1-4477-0260-3

Romania Through the Ages (2023)
ISBN
978-619-7742-19-0

www.ingramcontent.com/pod-product-compliance
Lightning Source LLC
LaVergne TN
LVHW010909200726